BREAKING
CHAINS

BY LAUREN ROSKILLY

TABLE OF CONTENTS

ABOUT THE AUTHOR

Lauren is a mum of two beautiful children and lives in Sussex, England. She became a born- again Christian in 2004.
Her qualifications include a BA Hons in Health and social care, a diploma in CBT and an accredited Life Coach certification, amongst others.

She is transparent about her past ups and downs with mental health, depression, anxiety and self- harm.
Since she was 14 years old, she has been through many valleys, trials and storms with her physical and mental health including, depression, anxiety, self- harm and attempted suicide. But God helped her to learn to change her focus from negativity and her limitations to focusing on God and His promises instead.

In 2018 God asked her to write a book, at the time she didn't know what it was to be about, but over the following few years this was revealed.

During a desperate time of prayer, God reminded Lauren of Jeremiah 29:1, she couldn't believe that He had plans to prosper her and give her a future, but a few years on it was clear that the pain that she experienced would be used for a purpose and the mess had become the message. Her story was used for good; for God's glory and to help others on their own journey. In 2019 she began her blog and 'Mindful of Christ' was born. Then in 2020, She was prompted to start writing that first book.

WHAT'S AVAILABLE FOR YOU?

Do you need help to break physical, emotional and/ or spiritual chains and to step into the freedom, identity and the purpose that God has for your life?
As a Coach, Lauren can help, guide and support you to achieve just this!

Do you need guidance, teaching & support with business, ministry and entrepreneurial start- up needs?
As a Mentor, Lauren can help you with these needs too!

"Done for you" services are also available, which includes (not limited to) editing, content writing and design. So, if you don't have enough time in the day, you have a deadline to meet or these tasks are simply just not for you, then check out these services.

- Book your FREE coaching/mentoring call: calendly.com/mindfulofchrist/book
- For more information on the above, check out the website: www.mindfulofchrist.net
- 'Biblical Affirmations' & 'How to Practice Biblical Mediation' freebie head here: mindfulofchrist.net/freebies

The following books are also available on the Mindful of Christ website and on Amazon:

COURSE FOR INDIVIDUALS & SMALL GROUPS

CHRISTIAN BASED COGNITIVE BEHAVIOURAL THERAPY

How to become mindful of Christ

LAUREN ROSKILLY

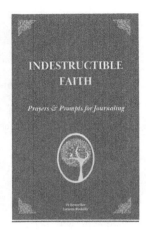

INDESTRUCTIBLE FAITH

Prayers & Prompts for Journaling

#1 Bestseller
Lauren Roskilly

INTRODUCTION

Do you know about AND experience true freedom within your life?

The kind of freedom where you live in peace and joy (most of the time anyway- you are human... aren't you?!)
The kind of freedom that strengthens you and helps you to deal with life here on Earth and everything that comes with it.
The kind of freedom that brings you affirmation and reassurance. The kind of freedom where your faith is strong, hope, joy and peace are present and you love & know you are loved too!

If your answer is "yes," I'm so pleased and happy for you! But this book may not be for you! (However, I encourage you to share it with someone who may benefit from it.)

If your answer is "no," then read on.
Perhaps there are "chains" in your life that are stopping you from experiencing this freedom.
These *chains* can be physical, emotional or spiritual.

Physical chains can include; behaviours, habits, illness or maybe situational.
Emotional chains can include; thoughts (the way you think), beliefs (about yourself and your capabilities), responses to situations (stress and/or depression), toxic feelings and emotions (those that have a tendency to consume your thoughts and perhaps your life).
Spiritual chains can include; beliefs (again), temptation, forgiveness, guilt and distractions.

If you can recognise and struggle with just a few or all of these, then this book was written for you!

"I wish I could promise you a trouble- free life as a Christian. Christ did not, and I cannot. The Christian life is not easy. You will need to work at staying connected to God. There is a devil, the enemy who will do all he can to break your connection with God." (John, J, 2009)

You are most likely well aware of this! We can't stop some things from happening but you *can* learn how to deal with and tackle them. There are other things that may happen that could develop over the years into those restrictive chains and hold you hostage.

But it is time to break those chains and live in the freedom (and purpose) that God has for you!

N.B I do not claim to have it all together, I'm not perfect, we are all on a journey! Just let me share with you what God taught me on my own journey of growth and development so you too can break those chains and live in the freedom that He *has* promised you.

In my distress I prayed to the Lord, and the Lord answered me and set me free. Psalm 118:5

In this book the scriptures used are all from the New Living Translation (NLT).

ESSENTIAL FIRST STEPS

Breaking those chains and making changes has to start somewhere! It starts with us! It starts with you! Yes God created you, but you weren't put on this Earth as His puppet! He gave each of us freewill. God- the Father, Son and Holy Spirit (the Trinity) are here to guide you through life here on earth and into eternity.

Just as you may use a map, sat nav or your own sense of direction to direct your path, you still need to decide which one you will use! You need to decide on your destination and you need to decide how you are going to get there. It comes down to making decisions and choices.

Everything that has been invented has to start with an idea or a thought. Then after that thought occurs, decisions need to be made. Do you ignore your thoughts and ideas, act on them, decide how you will achieve them or put them into action and make that first step?

You have obviously already made the decision to own and read this book. So, congratulations for making that first step!

The **3As** are an important part of these first steps.

1. Awareness

Before chains can be broken or changes can be made you need to have a look at what it is that may need "breaking" or changing.

✎   **Activity:**

Look again at the list in the 'Introduction' of the physical, emotional and spiritual chains. Write down everything you can think of that is or could be:

- **Burdening you**
- **Increasing stress levels**
- **Bringing on toxic emotions**
- **Consuming your thoughts**
- **Impacting behaviours & decisions**

2. Acceptance

There are two things in life that need to be acknowledged and accepted.

i.   Control and responsibility.

There are inevitably consequences to actions. For instance, if your behaviour or actions have had an impact on a situation or on someone else, then you need to spend time and think about what could possibly be done to rectify that.

For example; If you have a situation or an illness, is there anything you can do to improve it?
Once you've tried everything you can do or there isn't anything you can do to change it then perhaps acceptance is what is needed here. Or if something was said or done that upset someone else then an apology needs to be made.

ii.   God's help.

Do you fully understand and accept that God is the one that is there for you *all* the time? He loves you unconditionally and will take care of you.

But God showed his great love for us by sending Christ to die for us while we were still sinners.
Romans 5:8

And this same God who takes care of me will supply all your needs from his glorious riches, which have been given to us in Christ Jesus.
Philippians 4:19

Accepting that change needs to be made and that you have chains that need breaking may be really hard to do! But as you go through this book, you will learn how to address, overcome and accept situations and circumstances that you are in or are beyond your control. You will also learn how to know, in your heart, what God says about you, that He is there to help you and has provided the Holy Spirit and all His fruits; peace, love, joy and freedom for you too.

3. Action

Next, it's time to get into action!

Remembering that the Trinity is your Guide! Pray, ask Him for help. You don't have to go through life alone: He is with you and sees you everywhere you go.

What's more, I am with you, and I will protect you wherever you go. One day I will bring you back to this land. I will not leave you until I have finished giving you everything I have promised you."
Genesis 28:15

Be specific with your prayers too, see the chapter 'Pray'. Ask Him for help in each of the areas that you have uncovered in the previous activity. Then it's time to act on each! The rest of the book will help you with this action to break chains.

RELATIONSHIP IS KEY

Having a relationship with God and loving Him and others is the key factor in breaking any chains that are binding, preventing or limiting you from the fullness and freedom that God has for you.

I am not saying that if you have chains and barriers you do not have a relationship with the Father, Son and Holy Spirit! We live on this fallen earth and difficulties; trials and problems are inevitable. It's *how* you either deal or live with these that matters. You can experience all of these hardships but still know, experience and live in the freedom, love, joy and peace that God has for you and the basis of this is a relationship with God.

There may be areas that you still may struggle with that could be preventing you from living in the full freedom that you and His children are **ALL** entitled to and promised..

The first and second commandments are the core of the entire Holy Bible, all of the laws given to Moses in the book of Exodus and what Jesus, Himself, teaches.

Jesus replied: "'Love the Lord your God with all your heart and with all your soul and with all your mind.'' This is the first and greatest
commandment. And the second is like it: 'Love your neighbour as yourself.' All the Law and the Prophets hang on these two commandments."
Matthew 22:37-40

You have been given freewill and therefore, it is your *choice* to live by these commandments, to grow your love for God and other people too.

It's up to you!

15

Growing in love with anyone is done by the building of relationships.

There are 6 main factors in which you can do to do just this:

1. Taking interest

In God: you can do this through reading the Holy Bible. The whole Bible is God given, the authors were guided by Him and the Holy Spirit (2 Timothy 3:16) on what to write and so the texts and words will reflect His personality. Then there are the gospels, Matthew, Mark, Luke and John, which show you first hand at what Jesus was like, who He is, how He acts, speaks and behaves.

In others*:* Get to know them, ask questions in order to find out about them; their likes, dislikes, background, beliefs, etc.

2. Acceptance & Respect

For God: By knowing Him, His ways, words and promises we can learn to accept who He is and by doing this, your respect for Him will grow too. He has so many names! We read in the Bible that He is the Beginning and the End, the Alpha and Omega, Creator, Way maker, Promise keeper, Light, King and Lord, this list goes on! When God is respected, He's not being taken advantage of; for instance, not seeing Him as a genie who will grant every wish. He is your Father and as a Father He knows what is best for all of His children. You will be disciplined but you are also loved, cherished, adopted into His family and accepted by Him too!

For Others: The verse "do to others what you would have them do to you" (Matt 7:12) is based on this. If you want to receive acceptance and respect then you need to treat others this way too.

We can do this through honesty, integrity, compassion and by not gossiping or thinking we're any better than anyone else. Remaining humble is important! This works the other way too, all people are equal, so it's important to know your identity and worth too (see the chapter on 'Perception').

3. Positive Regard

Of God: This is having a full acceptance of God. It's about accepting who God is, even when the world is falling apart around you and you are enduring severe difficulties etc. It's knowing He is God and He is your saviour at all times and through all situations. Though this may be harder to do in practice! (As you read on, you will discover ways that will help you to get to this point of full acceptance.)

Of Others: To accept and support other people. For instance; who they are, their beliefs and behaviours. Love, forgiveness and not being judgemental is important here and is encouraged to be practised. Check out the chapter 'prune' for more on this.

4. Basic needs (companionship, affection, and emotional support)

To God: He wants to come in and eat with you. He knocks at the door of your heart (Revelation 3:20). He wants to sit at your table and be part of your life. You just need to let him in and include Him in it.

To Others: You weren't designed to be alone (Genesis 2:18) therefore you need to be a good companion towards others. Honour and respect, again, are important here (Romans 12:10) as is being kind and compassionate (Ephesians 4:32) to each other. If someone needs emotional support, you are to be there to provide it. Remembering, to love all your neighbours! We can do this by listening and simply "being there" for someone. Do remember this doesn't mean you are to do absolutely anything and everything for everyone. You may need to apply boundaries. It's important to remember that your basic needs are important too. You are important and if you don't take care of yourself you will not be of any use or help for anyone else! It's like the safety procedure on an aeroplane; it's paramount that you put your own mask on first!

    You can't help and support others if you are running out of oxygen yourself!

5. Reciprocity (give/ time)

To God: He wants you to spend time with Him. Not just once a week at church. He wants you to have that 1:1 alone time with Him. Jesus was a great example of this. The amount of times He left the disciples to go and spend time with God (Luke 6:12/ Matthew 6:6 etc.) You can use this example too.
Make it a priority to set aside time to be alone with God. **To Others:** I believe this to be one of the core components of a relationship. If you love someone or want to grow that love, the more time you need to spend with that person. Then, as that love grows that 'need' will switch to 'want' and you will start to *want* to spend time with that person. Either way, giving time to someone is a gift that is more precious than any other.

6. Communication

With God: He wants you to call out and talk to Him and He wants to be part of your life. He wants you to ask him questions and He wants to respond and talk to you too! (Jeremiah 33:3) Therefore, listening is also an important part of communication. There are different ways in which you can hear from God: Sitting quietly and listening for His small voice (1 Kings 19:11-

18

13), reading scripture (2 Timothy 3:16-17), prophecy and discernment (1 Corinthians 12:10), visions (Acts 2:17-18), angels (Luke 1:26-38), through creation (Psalm 19:12) and circumstances (Revelation 3:8). **With Others:** We are to talk and listen to others too. It might be obvious, but how much do we both talk and listen, I mean really listen? (See the Chapter on Prayer).

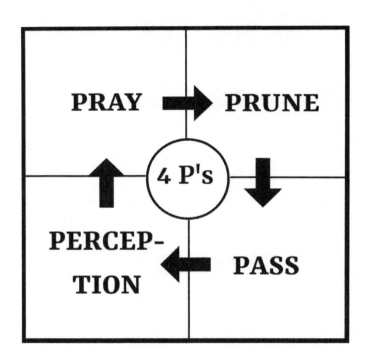

The Four P's are:

      1. Pray (communication)
      2. Prune (eliminating hindrances)
      3. Pass (to Jesus and let go)
      4. Perception (beliefs and focus)

All of which are paramount in breaking chains. Both exclusively and collectively. Individually and combined.
Each part has their own important part to play and yet they are intertwined with one another too. There is also a bonus P; Praise, which is just as important as the rest and should be applied throughout and at all times.
Each 'P' has a chapter of its own which explains it's meaning in more depth and includes activities for you too.
The action of and application of these activities will lead you towards the fullness and freedom that God does have for you.

The creation looks forward to the day when it will join God's children in glorious freedom from death and decay.
Romans 8:21

And you will know the truth, and the truth will set you free."
John 8:32

So, Christ has truly set us free. Now make sure that you stay free, and don't get tied up again in slavery to the law.
Galatians 5:1

PRAY

Prayer is the essential first step. In fact, it's not just the first, but second, third, fourth, well, actually it needs to be the core of your life when you are living as a believer and Child of God. I can't reiterate enough the importance of prayer! As briefly mentioned earlier, in the Relationship chapter, God wants to be part of your lives, He wants you to have a relationship with Him and communication is a key component in this. Jesus demonstrated the importance of prayer and communication with God and you are to learn from Him and take a leaf out of Jesus' book! Literally, yes?!

So, let's take a look at Jesus' explanation in Matthew 6.

Jesus says that praying isn't a "show" (Verse 5-6). It's a personal thing that is meant to be between you and God; it's an intimate time you have together with the Lord.

Jesus then goes on to explain that you shouldn't babble or repeat yourself when you pray (verse 7). There's no need to go off on those long-winded sentences and prayers. Just get straight to the point. Know what you want to say and say it. I'm sure He would enjoy having a casual chat with you too! I do, especially whilst walking, cooking or cleaning!

After Jesus has finished telling His audience, you, how not to pray, He goes on to say how it should be done. He gets straight to the point and demonstrates it through the Lord's prayer:

"'Our Father in heaven, hallowed be your name,
your kingdom come, your will be done, on earth as it is in heaven.
Give us today our daily bread. And forgive us our debts, as we
also have forgiven our debtors. And lead us not into temptation,
but deliver us from the evil one. (verse 9-18)

This prayer begins by addressing God by name; Father, and acknowledging His Holiness. He is your father, but you also need to remember His Greatness and supremacy too.

Next, this prayer is asking that God's will, will be done. This is a key factor in how to live our lives. Asking Him for guidance and that His will is done and not yours.

'Our daily bread' is Jesus, your sustenance, He is your spiritual food. You can be fed through the word of God; the Holy Bible. He is the one that will sustain you. Getting to know Him by reading the word is the only way in which your hunger will be fed.

Are you hungry for God and His word? Do you want to feel full?

The next part of the prayer is a reminder to ask for forgiveness. We are all sinners saved by grace, but nevertheless we all need forgiving. Then, on the flip side of this we need to *accept* His forgiveness too.

Have you accepted that you have been forgiven?

In addition to all of this you are to forgive others as well. Having the *chain* of unforgiveness in your heart can prevent you from living in the true freedom that God has for you (more of this in the chapter, Prune).

Next, the Lord's prayer encourages us to ask God to lead us away from temptation. This is a sure example that temptation can, in fact, be resisted. I'm not saying it's easy or simple, because it isn't! Any human being on this earth has been and will be tempted from time to time. Even Jesus was tempted when He was in the desert (Matthew 4:1)! But, that is another reason why prayer is so important; God can help, guide and

24

deliver you! But He does like you to speak to Him and ask for this.

This prayer is a great example of intentional praying. It's simple, straight to the point and heartfelt. This is exactly how we are to pray.

Praying in the Spirit is also an important part of prayer! The Holy Spirit gives us plenty of other abilities too (1 Corinthians 12:10), but this verse is specifically talking about tongues and prophecy. These come about when you have been baptised by the Holy Spirit, which is something you may already have received but in addition to this you can ask God for specific ones too. When you do this, you will come to know and understand the full power that God has for you.

> **I didn't know he was the one, but when God sent me to baptize with water, he told me, 'The one on whom you see the Spirit descend and rest is the one who will baptize with the Holy Spirit.'**
> **John 1:33**

Baptism of water is different from the baptism of the Spirit. It is something that *all* believers can receive. It is your promise from God.

> **Peter replied, "Each of you must repent of your sins and turn to God, and be baptized in the name of Jesus Christ for the forgiveness of your sins. Then you will receive the gift of the Holy Spirit. This promise is to you, to your children, and to those far away—all who have been called by the Lord our God." Acts 2:38-9**

Speaking in tongues is the conversation our spirit has directly with the Holy Spirit. It's nothing to be afraid of, as you may think or feel. Though this fear or wariness is most likely to do with the unknown, not knowing about what it is and that it is different

25

from anything else you've heard of before. But it is good to remember that this is an important part of your walk with God. It's simply speaking in another language. The reason it's important is because it's a "direct line" to God. The enemy knows your thoughts and what you say to others and even to God in prayer, but when we pray in the spirit; in tongues, the enemy cannot understand what is being said (1 Corinthians 14:14). Yes, I know, we may not necessarily know either, but that's ok. When we speak in tongues we are edifying ourselves, building on our spiritual growth and strengthening our relationship with God (1 Corinthians 14:4).

Praying in tongues is also helpful when you simply just don't know what to pray. For instance, when you're desperate, anxious, exhausted, etc. This is when the Spirit intercedes for you.

> **And the Holy Spirit helps us in our weakness. For example, we don't know what God wants us to pray for. But the Holy Spirit prays for us with groanings that cannot be expressed in words.**
> **Romans 8:26**

So, you can see that both prayer in your own language and in tongues are both very important for your Spiritual growth and relationship with God.

Activity:
Think about how much time you can realistically commit to the Lord on a daily or weekly basis?
Then:
- **Write down your answers**
- **Add to you diary/ calendar**
- **Set regular reminders**

PRUNE (ELIMINATE HINDRANCES)

Prune, or pruning is the next step. The definition of this is to eliminate hindrances. In other words, those 'things' in your life that are holding you back from living in the freedom and purpose that God has for you. Those 'things,' could be distractions, unforgiveness, behaviours, actions and/ or habits.

> So, Christ has truly set us free. Now make sure that you stay free, and don't get tied up again in slavery to the law.
> Galatians 5:1

This scripture is for all of his children. That's YOU! Not just a chosen few believers, but everyone who has accepted Christ as their saviour; this freedom *is* for you!
Now, the question is are you living in this every day?
Chances are, if you are reading this, you may need a little help. This is where the pruning comes in, along with the other P's!

John 15 is the *core* of this Chapter.

> "I am the true grapevine, and my Father is the gardener. ²He cuts off every branch of mine that doesn't produce fruit, and he prunes the branches that do bear fruit so they will produce even more. ³ You have already been pruned and purified by the message I have given you. ⁴Remain in me, and I will remain in you. For a branch cannot produce fruit if it is severed from the vine, and you cannot be fruitful unless you remain in me. ⁵"Yes, I am the vine; you are the branches. Those who remain in me, and I in them, will produce much fruit. For apart from me you can do nothing. ⁶ Anyone who does not remain in me is thrown away like a useless branch and withers. Such branches are gathered into a pile to be burned. ⁷But if you remain in me and my words remain in you, you may ask for anything you want, and it will be granted! ⁸When you produce much fruit, you are my true disciples. This brings

great glory to my Father. ⁹"I have loved you even as the Father has loved me. Remain in my love. ¹⁰When you obey my commandments, you remain in my love, just as I obey my Father's commandments and remain in his love. ¹¹I have told you these things so that you will be filled with my joy. Yes, your joy will overflow! ¹²This is my commandment: Love each other in the same way I have loved you. ¹³There is no greater love than to lay down one's life for one's friends. ¹⁴You are my friends if you do what I command. ¹⁵I no longer call you slaves, because a master doesn't confide in his slaves. Now you are my friends, since I have told you everything the Father told me. ¹⁶You didn't choose me. I chose you. I appointed you to go and produce lasting fruit, so that the Father will give you whatever you ask for, using my name. ¹⁷This is my command: Love each other.

John 15: 1-17

You can see straight away that God, the Father, is also a gardener. You are the vine and He takes care of you. Imagine being in a garden and pruning your trees and plants; getting rid of all those weeds and the dying or already dead branches that are preventing its health and growth. Well, that is exactly what the Father does for you!

He wants you to produce good fruit and get rid of the bad stuff. He wants you to keep producing that good fruit too! The 'good fruit,' is love, joy, peace, hope, kindness, patience, goodness, gentleness and self- control, these are the fruit of the Spirit (Galatians 5:22-3). The more we abide in, have a relationship with, look to and be filled with the God, the Father, Son and Holy Spirit the more likely we are to grow and harvest that good fruit.

But why would you want that?

Because the more 'good fruit' you have the more you will be able to handle life; the more aligned with God you are, the more resilient you become, the more you can grow, both spiritually, emotionally and personally. Then, as a result of this, the freer you become too! You *can* be free from the 'things' that hold you back. With your Father at the core of your being, you can do pretty much anything, according to His purpose and plan (verse 5 & Philippians 4:13). When you are apart from Him, you are pretty much useless (ouch, that hurts, right?!) but it's true (verse 6 and 7). With Him we can thrive, without Him we may as well be put into the compost heap! So, assess yourself and your life and let God be your gardener. He loves you and all He wants is for you to remain in Him and love Him too (verse 9-10).

In order to do this though, you need to prune, remove, the weeds and dead leaves that aren't meant to be part of your life. This can be done through repentance, forgiveness and eliminating distractions and behaviours.

Repentance isn't necessarily something you do just once. Ideally, in a perfect world, it would be, but, as you well know this world is not perfect (it was in the beginning though) and you are human! Repentance, like pruning, is something you may need to do again and again and hopefully not for the same thing, but as I said, it does happen, so give yourself a break! You are saved by the Fathers forgiveness and grace! That is why Jesus died on the cross for you. Your sins have been forgiven and you don't need to feel shame or guilt anymore. On that cross it was done and finished (John 19:30)! But, if there *is* something in your life that keeps rearing its ugly head, then you do need to take that responsibility and get rid of it. This is where repentance comes in. The definition of repentance is, "the fact of showing that you are sorry for something wrong that you have done" (Oxford, 2022).

Remember when you were a child and a parent, adult or guardian said to you "say sorry" then you would but perhaps you didn't truly mean it, so they would say to you "say sorry properly!" Well, that's what it's like. You need to sincerely be sorry, from your heart. If you are, you will have every intention not to do it again. That is the real and true definition of repentance.

✎   **Activity:**
Have a good think and ask God to reveal to you if you have anything in your lives that needs true repentance.
Write down whatever comes to mind.
Pray. Repent and ask your Father for forgiveness. Then let it go.

Your prayer could go something like this:
"Father, thank you for your forgiveness. Thank you for what Jesus went through on the cross for me. I'm sorry for _____. Please forgive me and help me not to do or repeat _____ again. Help me to be more like Jesus. Thank you. In His might name, Amen"

Unforgiveness is another weed or 'bad fruit' that you need to get rid of too. Having any unforgiveness in your heart doesn't affect the person you are not forgiving, but what it does affect is you, your relationship with God and it can limit and restrict the freedom that you could potentially be living in. Unforgiveness is such a bad fruit, it has more effect on the person harbouring it. If you want to be forgiven for your sins and live in that freedom the Father has for you then you absolutely need to forgive others too.

"If you forgive those who sin against you, your heavenly Father will forgive you. But if you refuse to forgive others, your Father will not forgive your sins.
Matthew 6:14-15

Forgiveness is a matter of your heart and mind. Firstly, you need to decide if you are ready to fully forgive. Then you need to release that hold it has on you and give those thoughts and resentments up and let go of them (See the activity in the chapter 'Pass,' for more on this). When you have fully forgiven the person or God who needs your forgiveness, you will notice that a weight *will* be lifted from you and you *will* feel a lot lighter and freer too. It can also be helpful to tell the person or God, too, if possible. It may be a new beginning and bridges can start to be built.

Distractions can also have an impact on you and your relationship and walk with your Father. What you focus on is key. Is your focus on God, the Father and gardener or are you distracted? Maybe by a relationship, project, social media, Netflix, work... the list can go on. There is nothing wrong with any of these things at all, but when they become a distraction or take you away from your Father and your main purpose that He has for you, that's when it could perhaps be a problem. You need to recognise and check yourself and see if there are any distractions that need pruning from your life. If there is something that you can take hold of then it is up to you to cut these back and remove them from your life.

Though this may not always be simple to do. Sometimes, we can't always just "get rid" of our distractions. For instance; a long-term sickness. When this is the case, the answer could be about your focus and the object of attention.

There was a woman, Florence Chadwick, who in 1952 attempted to swim 26 miles between Catalina Island and the

32

California coastline. She had a boat travelling alongside her, for safety. Chadwick was doing well and had swam half way before getting tired, her destination was in sight and so she persevered. But then the fog came down and she could no longer see her destination, all she saw was the fog, she grew tired and eventually gave up and climbed aboard the boat. It wasn't until afterwards that she discovered that she was less than a mile away from her destination! Later, she attempted the same course again, this time when the fog came down, she had an image in her mind of the coastline that she was heading for. Low and behold, she reached the destination!

We need to keep our eyes fixed on the goal, that is Jesus and the promise of eternal life.

I don't mean to say that I have already achieved these things or that I have already reached perfection. But I press on to possess that perfection for
which Christ Jesus first possessed me. No, dear brothers and sisters, I have not achieved it, but I focus on this one thing: Forgetting the past and
looking forward to what lies ahead, I press on to reach the end of the race and receive the heavenly prize for which God, through Christ Jesus, is calling us.
Philippians 3:12-14

See more on how to fix your eyes on the goal; Jesus, in the chapter, 'Perception.'

Activity:

Think about the following questions and write down your answers.

- Is there anyone that you haven't yet forgiven?
- What, if anything, is distracting you from the Father, Son and Holy Spirit?

Ask God to help you with forgiveness and/ or to get rid of these distractions and to help you to keep your focus on Him.

PASS (TO JESUS AND LET GO!)

The third step, Pass, follows on from Prune well. You will give to Jesus all those pieces of your life that you have just pruned, including any thoughts and worries that are keeping you in chains or are preventing you from living in the full freedom that God has for you.

You may know that once a gardener has finished his weeding and pruning, he then gets rid of it all, either on the compost heap or in the garden waste bin. He doesn't keep or hold onto any of the parts he's cut or pulled away. Right?

You need to do the same. It's time to get rid of it all! This means to get rid of all of those thoughts, worries, behaviours, habits, perhaps certain relationships. The Lord wants us to trust Him and to do so with *every* part of our lives.

> Trust in the LORD with all your heart; do not depend
> on your own understanding. Seek his will in all you do,
> and he will show you which path to take.
> Proverbs 3:5-6

Notice the word 'all,' twice it is mentioned here, "*all* your heart" and "*all* you do" not just some of it, but all!

I know this seems easier said than done! You may know this verse and know this is how you need to be. Perhaps you do trust Him fully in some areas of your life. But are there any grey areas? Are there pieces of your life or ways of being that you still like or need to be in control over or that has control over you? These are the pieces that need to be handed over to God and let go of, I mean *fully* let go of.

I went through this process myself. I used to struggle; I believe now that where I didn't have any control over the

past health condition I had, there wasn't anything I or the doctors could do and so that need to be in control of other areas of my life was almost understandable. I felt I needed to be in control of something! But this led to me making some poor decisions and one day I "woke up," I realised what was happening, but ultimately that need for control had impacted my whole life and even took me off course. At the time I had convinced myself it was all ok, but I was heading down the wrong path and needed to head back to the path that God had already mapped out for me.

Sometimes, it can be your own thoughts and decisions, other times the enemy likes to make us believe that certain situations, behaviours, thoughts and beliefs are actually ok and they aren't a problem or affecting anyone (see the chapter, Perception). But the question is, does it align with God and His will? We need to listen carefully and read the word of God, the Holy Bible and if our thoughts and behaviours do not align with this then, they are not right and we need to do something about it. If we don't we can end up further down the wrong path or even get off of the track completely and we can get lost in the dark woods and it can become even harder to find the way back (still speaking metaphorically, but you catch my drift?!)

I needed to let God into *all* the areas of my life, get back to Him and get back to the Word.

Do you?

In order to find the right path, you will need to give up yourself, worries, toxic thoughts and beliefs, behaviours and control. You need to surrender. This means to give up yourself and your will and let go of those pieces of your life that are holding you back from freedom. By letting go of control and worries and putting your full trust in the Father, Son and Holy Spirit. Not just in your mind, but in your heart, soul and spirit too! Take that map, aka, the Holy Bible & the Holy Spirit and find the correct path. He will guide you; you just need to ask Him. Ask Him for help. Ask Him to help you get rid of those chains. Ask Him for His will to be done in each and all areas of your life (Matthew 6:10).

Then once you have achieved this you will see, if you haven't already, that He has a purpose and plan for you!

> For I know the plans I have for you," says the LORD.
> "They are plans for good and not for disaster, to give
> you a future and a hope.
> Jeremiah 29:11

Ask Him about them. They are so much more that you can ask or begin to imagine. They are better than what you may have had planned for your own life.

So let go! Let go of all those chains that are holding you back from the freedom that God has for you. The activity below will help you with this.

🖋 **Activity:**
Try out any or all of the following:

- **Imagine you are carrying a bag full of rocks. Each rock symbolises each worry and concern you have. You are walking down a path carrying this bag and it's heavy and weighing you down. Then you turn around and see Jesus. You open the bag, take out each rock, one at a time looking and knowing what each one is and physically hand them over to Him, naming them as they go. Then thank Jesus for taking them from you. No longer are you carrying the rocks or cares, they are in Jesus' hands now.**

38

- **You could write them onto small bits of paper individually then screw them up and act out the above scenario. Then throw them away.**
- **Otherwise, if you have a cross, you can write down each care and pin or nail them onto it.**

You may find you need to check yourself regularly over the course of your life and re- surrender and re- submit to God. It's good to have a "clear out" once in a while. Like you would with your own homes and/ or gardens. Think of your spiritual health as something to upkeep and maintain. Make sure you are letting go of those parts that you don't need to hold on to and give yourself to God and His will on a daily basis.

PERCEPTION

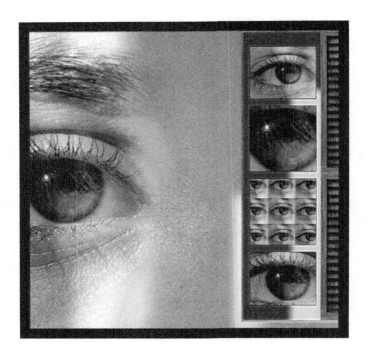

The fourth step is Perception. This is to do with your view and opinion of the world and yourself. How you think and your beliefs can have a huge impact on how you live your life.

- Are you a "glass is half empty" person?
- Do you tend to be negative about yourself and situations?
- Do you find yourself focusing on the bad parts of life?
- Do you know in your heart that you are fearfully and wonderfully made (Psalm 139:14) or do you say things like "I'm not good enough", "no one loves me", "I'm too old or too young", "I'm not talented enough", "I don't have enough experience"?
- Is your perception limiting you and prevent you from living life in the fullness and freedom that God *does* have for you?

Lots of questions here. Take some time to reflect on these and answer them truthfully.

This perspective can also be known as the 'limiting beliefs' or 'Imposter Syndrome.' But I can't ask you 'do you have limiting beliefs?' because the chances are, you may not be aware that these are limiting you or holding you back; they are your truths and perhaps your reality.
According to psychology, there are 5 different types of "Imposters":

1. Perfectionist: Fixates on their flaws and can never be good enough.
2. Superhero: Feels as though they need to work as hard as possible.
3. Expert: Underrates their knowledge and wisdom and always wants to learn more & more.

4. Natural Genius: Sets high goals and is upset when they don't achieve these at the first attempt.
5. Soloist: Very independent people who find it hard to ask for help or assistance.

Can you relate to any of these? Perhaps you have lived your whole life believing and doing these things. In which case, you may not know a different way of being or if it is even possible to live and believe differently at all!

Don't copy the behaviour and customs of this world, but let God transform you into a new person by changing the way you think. Then you will learn to know God's will for you, which is good and pleasing and perfect.
Romans 12:2

This verse in Romans is good news for you! Your mind, perspective, thoughts and beliefs **can** be transformed! Most importantly, God can help you to do this. So, start off with prayer. Ask Him to help you to change your mind and perspective. If you can be specific and you know each individual limitation then offer them individually to God, asking him to change them, so you can be free from these and know and understand how God sees you, not just in your mind, but in your heart also.

It is useful to understand where these thoughts and beliefs have come from. They can be from one or a combination of the following:

- God
- Satan
- Other people
- Ourselves- including our background, past and current situations

These thoughts or voices in your head, which most of the time can sound or feel like they are your own. But the reality is, they aren't all your own! For instance, if another person has told you in the past "you're useless at (fill in the blank)" let's say drawing. Those words may have stuck in your head and now 5, 10, 20 years on you still believe that you can't draw and you don't do it at all even though it was in fact something you used to enjoy. But, what if it wasn't actually true and all that time you believed that it was?

Have a look at the questions and your answers from the beginning of this chapter and ask yourself where each of them could have stemmed from. Then challenge them and ask yourself, "is this belief/ thought actually the truth?"

What if you knew and truly believed in your heart everything God, through the scriptures, says about the world and you? How different would your life be?

Have a look at the following *truth* statements:

1. God loved the world so much that he gave his only Son, Jesus, and that whoever believes in him will not perish but will have eternal life. (John 3:16)
2. God chose & loves *you*! (Deuteronomy 10:15)
3. He adopted *you* as His Son or daughter for His will and His delight. (Ephesians 1:5)
4. *You* are made in the image of Jesus. (Romans 8:29)
5. *You* are fearfully and wonderfully made! (Psalm 139:14)

Do you believe these statements yet?
Look in the Holy Bible and find more of these. Meditate on them and the scriptures and apply them to your life. Repetition is key! The more you hear and see something the higher chance you

have at moving the statement from your mind into your heart, this is why Biblical meditation can be powerful. (See how to access your free *'Biblical Affirmations'* poster and *'How to practice Biblical Meditation'* in the 'What's Available for You' chapter.)

To help you to tackle and overcome deep, embedded negative beliefs there is an activity below. I did this exact activity myself, years ago and it literally changed my life! I no longer believe the old way of thinking and I'm not bound by those chains of limiting beliefs anymore. I now share it with any coaching client and anyone else that may need it too! So, if you struggle with those limiting thoughts and mindsets then I strongly recommend you complete this. You never know, it could change your life too!

Activity:
You will need: Paper, pen and pencil.

1. **Using your pencil. On the first line write down your negative statement/ belief. Write all the statements down that you experience, leaving 3 lines blank in between each.**
2. **Take your pen. Now you write a positive statement underneath the ones in pencil. (Use only positive words, not negative ones.**

E.g., "don't", "not", "no", "can't", and so on.) It needs to be the complete opposite of what you wrote in pencil.

44

For instance;

"I am stupid" would be followed by "I am good at many things." "I am alone" or "no one cares about me" would be followed by "God will never leave me or forsake me"

You can use truths from the Bible (see above example) and any others you can think of.

Write 2- 3 positive statements to counteract each of the negative ones.

3. For one week, read your piece(s) of paper from top to bottom- the negative followed by the positive. (30secs5mins/ day)
4. After a week, get an eraser and rub out the negative pencilled statements.
5. For one more week, Read the paper from top to bottom.

So, just 30 seconds to a few minutes a day for two weeks could break those mindset chains, free you of limiting beliefs and change your whole outlook on life, so you can get back onto the right path and purpose that Jesus has for you.

Do you think that it's worth it?!

Another element of perception is what our attention and focus is fixed on. "Check in" with yourself now and on a regular basis, especially when you start worrying or recognise toxic thoughts and emotions creeping in. Notice what your focus is on. Ask yourself what you are paying attention to, "What is currently consuming or dominating my thoughts?"

"Anyone who listens to my teaching and follows it is wise, like a person who builds a house on solid rock. Though the rain comes in torrents and
the floodwaters rise and the winds beat against that house, it won't collapse because it is built on bedrock. But anyone who hears my teaching and
doesn't obey it is foolish, like a person who builds a house on sand. When the rains and floods come and the winds beat against that house, it will collapse with a mighty crash."
Matt 7:24-27

In the above scripture these storms represent life's difficulties, problems and circumstances and Jesus is telling you that if you build your life on the rock, which is Him, and keep your focus on Him, you are building a firm foundation, one that can withstand the storms of life. By doing so, you can build up resilience against them, grow closer to God and live in that freedom, peace, love and joy, no matter what is going on around you.

Imagine you are inside a house and there is a storm outside. The wind is blowing and the heavy rain is pounding on the windows. It's dark and the thunder and lightning sounds as though it is close by. You are inside, perhaps there's a cosy fire lit, keeping you warm, but you are sitting on the sofa and Jesus is sitting right next to you. You aren't staring out of the window feeling fearful, you are looking directly at Jesus and you are experiencing true love, joy and peace.

The storm (worries, concerns and distractions) may be going on around you and you are in the middle but you are looking at and are focused on Him instead.

So, you may need to grab hold of your thoughts and focus and consciously and intentionally change the direction you are looking in; turn your focus around and look towards Jesus.

PRAISE (BONUS 'P')

This bonus step, is one that you can and should be doing the whole way through both this process and throughout life! Praise is *so* important! There is never a time in which we should not be praising the Lord. It isn't something you do just when you are happy and life is going well, but continuously; at all times.

Therefore, let us offer through Jesus a continual sacrifice of praise to God, proclaiming our allegiance to his name.
Hebrews 13:15

Note the word 'continual.' This is because God is worthy of all praise. He is the creator of the earth, Lord of all, our father, the beginning and end, our saviour. It is because of Him we have eternity with Him on earth and in heaven. Wow! What a reason to be praising Him!

In addition to this, when you are thinking about positive, happy, nice, good things, which is quite obviously God, then there isn't room for much else in your mind and thoughts. So, when you are struggling in life; you have a difficult situation, experience problems and difficulties in life, then prayer and praise needs to be your first response.

What is the first thing you usually do when something bad occurs or you encounter difficulties?
Do you cry, moan, worry, drink, eat, break something, turn to someone else?
(There is nothing wrong with doing some of these, though perhaps one or two of them wouldn't be the best of responses!)

Lamenting is also important. This is because you do need to be able to recognise your feelings and emotions and when you do, offer them to God and ask Him for His help, guidance, peace, love, joy and freedom. Throughout the Psalms there are plenty of examples of lamentation. It is ok not to be ok! But, God wants you to share your struggles and sufferings with Him (1 Peter 5:7/ Matthew 11:28).

He also wants you to go to Him with prayer and praise too.

But I will give repeated thanks to the LORD, praising him to everyone. For he stands beside the needy, ready to save them from those who condemn them.
Psalm 109:30-1

So, meditate on and remember this verse too. Praise Him, He *will* stand with you!

THE ART OF REPETITION

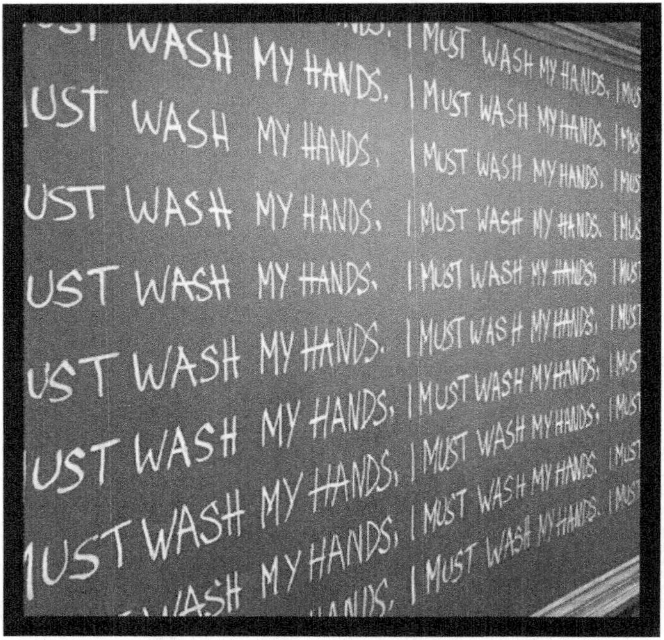

There has been one *reoccurring* factor that has been seen throughout the 4 P's and the bonus 'P' and that is 'Repetition.'

Prayer: this is something that should be an integral part of your life. It's about conversation with God, in order to keep that relationship with him going and growing then you need to talk to Him.

Prune: this is something that may need to be repeated as you go through life. Check in with yourself and see if there are any weeds that need pulling or branches that require cutting back.

Pass: this is something that you may have to repeat. Every time a worry or thought comes to mind, every time a new and difficult situation comes up, pass them over to God and let go of it.

Perception: this is something that may require changing in your life and mind. Repeat those affirmations, biblical meditations and statements you created from the activity.

Praise: this needs to be repeated daily, it needs to be consistent. Fill your heart and mind with praise and don't leave any room for negative thoughts or chains to reform.

It is with repetition that you can create new habits, behaviours and perspectives and create a new way of being with God at the *core*. Through this you can do what it says in Romans 12:2 and can truly be transformed by the renewing of your mind. Perseverance here is key. You've heard the saying "Rome wasn't built in a day!" It wasn't, it was a process and this may be too. Yes, God heals and yes people have changed instantly, thank you Lord for all those times! But, sometimes it can be a process. You may still have things that God is wanting you to learn, know, develop or grow in. Again, ask Him! When you are struggling with a certain situation or circumstance don't ask "why me?!" ask Him, "what can I learn from this?", "what is the point or reason for it?" and "what do you want me to do with this?"

It takes time to learn new things and create new habits. You may have heard that it takes 21 days to do so. But through thorough research and her new book 'Cleaning up your mental mess' Dr Caroline Leaf says that, "new thoughts are formed over 21 days, and these new thoughts are formed into habits within 63 days." Therefore, time, consistency and repetition are key factors.

When I first re- surrendered to God I wanted to know Him more, pray and read the Bible every single day and first thing in the morning, except doing so didn't come naturally to me, there were distractions, like sleep, children, breakfast, my phone and it was something that I simply wasn't used to doing first thing, when I woke up. So, I set my alarm, half an hour earlier, which had a note reminder on it, to read my Bible and pray. Then every time it went off I saw it, and I spent time in prayer and reading the Word before getting up in the morning. This was not easy to begin with. But as the days went by it became easier and easier. Then low and behold after a few months a habit was formed! Yes, it did seem a little religious to start with but the fact was my heart wanted it, I didn't do it because I felt I had to, I did it because I *wanted* to get to know Him and build that relationship up. (Notice, the *choice* that was made here; that choice is the beginning.) It went from intentional, to habit forming, to becoming second nature. I soon woke up and naturally began speaking with the Lord without needing that reminder anymore, before I even opened my eyes now I'm saying "good morning" to Him and spending that time praying before (and after) opening the Bible.

So, you can see that repetition was the beginning of my new relationship with God which led to breaking chains of distractions and old habits and beliefs to creating new ones and living in the freedom and purpose that God has and had pre planned and paved for me.

You can do this too, with this or anything. The more you practice and repeat something, like you would an instrument or a language, the better you become and the more natural it is for you to do whatever it is.

Read this book and check the activities out and repeat if and when necessary and you too will break those chains and live in the fullness, freedom, purpose, love, joy, peace *and* hope that God has for you!

REFERENCES

Cuncic, Arlin, 2022, 'What is Imposter Syndrome' on Very Well Mind, Available Online:
https://www.verywellmind.com/imposter-syndromeand-social-anxiety-disorder-4156469 Accesses 14/08/2022

John, J, 2009, 'Making the connection,' by Authentic Media, 9 Holdom Avenue, Milton Keynes, Bucks, MK1 1QR

Leaf, Dr. Caroline, 'Why mind-management is the solution to cleaning up your mental mess,' in Dr Leaf Switch on your Brain, Available online:
https://cdn.shopify.com/s/files/1/1810/9163/files/General_White_Paper_100720_final_version.pdf?v=1602124109 Accessed 13/08/2022

Leaf, Dr Caroline, Cleaning up your mental mess: 5 Simple, Scientifically Proven Steps to Reduce Anxiety, Stress and Toxic Thinking, Available: https://amzn.to/3Aknus9 Accessed 12/08/2022

Oxford, 2022, Repentance, Dictionaries, in Oxford Learner Dictionaries Available online:
https://www.oxfordlearnersdictionaries.com/definition/english/repentan ce#:~:text=repentance-
,noun,have%20done%20synonym%20contrition%2C%20remorse
Accessed 09/2022

Roskilly, Lauren, 2022, 'What is the Imposter Syndrome and how to overcome it?' in Blog Posts, *Mindful of Christ* Available Online: https://mindfulofchrist.net/what-is-imposter-syndrome-how-toovercome-it/ Accessed 14/08/2022

Breaking Chains

Printed in Great Britain
by Amazon